Poemisations

by
Dave Cook

Grosvenor House
Publishing Limited

This book is published by
Grosvenor House Publishing Ltd
Link House
140 The Broadway, Tolworth, Surrey, KT6 7HT.
www.grosvenorhousepublishing.co.uk

A CIP record for this book
is available from the British Library

Paperback ISBN 978-1-80381-438-4
Hardback ISBN 978-1-80381-563-3

In science one tries to tell people, in such a way as to be understood by everyone, something that no one ever knew before. But in poetry, it's the exact opposite. **Paul Dirac**

Poetry and slime are more fun to produce than to consume. **Felix the Helix**

Progress Report

David enjoyed a 1950s working-class upbringing in West Ham and an education in Canning Town, largely avoiding culture and beauty apart from Looney Tunes and the Northern Outfall Sewer embankment. He then spent many years in laboratories making chemicals with satisfactory progress.

Looking for something to do after forty years of science, and being an almost literature-free zone, he enrolled in a "Ways into Poetry" course. Surrounded by people steeped in English literature and the Classics, he came to appreciate that a creative and questioning science background can be a great resource for poetry. David has also been exposed to the Hungarian csardas, left-wing politics, divorce, heartbreak, 2-methyl-2-thiazoline, romantic love, joy, music, what you might call the downside of life, the philosophy of the Goon Show, Morris Dancers, a wonderful family, and Mad Magazine.

When asked about his approach to poetry he summarised:

(i)   Produce something a bit different
(ii) Don't worry too much about rules in poetry – if you want free verse, then have it!
(iii) Avoid workshopping – you may not like it but, for good or ill, it's all yours

CONTENTS

Poemisations #1

A Sort of Poetry

There must be a small part of spacetime
where the ukulele, sewage treatment,
Elmer Fudd, lost love and
paradise can coexist.

The Wonderful World of the Ukulele

All passion spent, weeping and praying, Trevor fell to his knees. Yes! Truly a musical triumph. Another Ukulele Night at the Pig and Whistle over.	Minutes before sleep overcame him, and enjoying the physical warmth after love, Nigel smiled to himself; no longer a virgin since buying that ukulele.
Ludwig van B looked up from the piano at the small guitar-shaped instrument on the shop wall; seeing the "Sold" sign, he sighed and thought of what just might have been.	With the dawn, came an awakening consciousness, the Ape realised that he had a weapon. Soon the male members of Tribe Two were to become the first ever victims of the ukulele.
It could have been the 15 minute ukulele solo, it could have been "Hip-Hop Sucks" crudely painted on his chosen instrument – either way Tarquin was doomed.	It was when Salieri first observed the ease with which young Amadeus mastered the ukulele's difficult Fmaj7 chord, that his interest in poisons took an unhealthy turn.
The endurance record for listening to the ukulele was set in 1976 by Jimmy-Bob Kronkite of Alabama, and stands at an unbelievable one minute seventeen seconds.	Only a humble snail, but playing hard-to-reach jazz chords rapidly while vigorously strumming, Felix was world famous for making it all look so f*****g difficult.

Early Autumn Sandwich: Part 1

A sandwich comprises two components
(i) a pair of sub-parallel plates of complex carbohydrate
flanking (ii) a chosen filling.

The filling, more interesting than the support structure
may be uniform of composition such as a
peanutty paste or a cheesy semi-solid
or, much better, of a varied and interesting texture,
not only in hardness, cohesion and durability
but in wetness, oiliness, spiciness or suspicious otherness.

Surrounding the sandwich could be
plates of a pleasant floral design,
an old-fashioned but still agreeable table,
two lovers, seated, juxtaposed at an angle of 135°
in a romantic location, say Budapest circa 1981
and a nearby potted palm, real or otherwise.

While biting through the outside structure into the delicious
contents of the inhomogeneous middle layer
the more romantic of the two lovers,
who will almost certainly be the man,
will experience a feeling
somewhere between the heart
and the stomach
of overwhelming love,
which he will wish to communicate
to the other.

The transmission of this information, however
will be compromised by a mayonnaise-coated salad leaf
adhering to his now-quivering cheek.

Although, like the sandwich, the female too comprises a somewhat
homogenous outer covering,
she has a more complex filling containing proteins, lipids,
memories, spleen, love, simmering passion for a Bulgarian
dancer, 1.5% calcium, fluids, music, viscera and
a fascinating ambivalence
to her male suitors,
rendering her irresistible.

A Model of the Universe

Having conceptualised a model of the Universe
from electrons to microbes to clusters of galaxies,
Barry descends the concrete steps in Canning Town
to search the forgotten dockland streets for ghosts,
faceless histories in duffle coats and something inside him,
something unknown, something about hope.

Having held the wisdom of civilisations at her fingertips
and learned well the history of mankind,
Paula moves the toys and the dirty washing
from the second-hand orange-brown sofa
and waits for her lover, where this will be
their timeless world for thirty seven minutes.

Having reflected on a world without meaning and
his own entrapment in visceral impermanence
Simon pulls on the worn, black leather boots and
the museum-grade, folk-dance costume
to perform to a fairly full house in Hoxton,
to come alive again as a sort of quiet god.

Having been blessed with the same capacity for joy,
more or less, as seven billion special others
Maria looks up from her teacup past her newly-dug patch,
breathing carbon dioxide out to the audience of brassicas,
dark leaves filled with droplets of early spring rain;
anticipating a future of photosynthetic pleasure.

Having inherited the magic potential for creation
chemically bonded into his chromosomes
Paul waits in the clinical mahogany Town Hall foyer,
prays in church in the stone and sterile silence,
listens, safe and whiteboarded, slick and powerpointed,
hardly aware that something has flown.

(You've Got To) Move Like Dali

At the age of 63, Veronica Grimsdale
was conferred a Ph.D.,

*At any point in this poem, one may affect an exaggerated look of surprise
and pretend to straighten an imaginary moustache.*

with which she signs her poetry.
She writes and worries endlessly

*In addition these movements may be followed by shrugs, expansive open
hand gestures and French or Spanish expletives, all executed while
imagining a beret and a striped sailor shirt.*

about poor homeless refugees
in tragic verse and sad spondees,

*Any public reader of this poem must not adopt the studied gravitas of
20th C British actORS or the energy of early 21st C urban hip-hop poets;
a monotonous drawl is preferred.*

but leaves my conscience wand'ring free.
For I have yearned too selfishly

*The reader may now don a white-faced clown outfit, ride a unicycle and
either juggle light bulbs or mime the poem.*

for someone also 63;
this poem I devote to she.

A Silver Bullet for the Moon

"For too long he sculpted stars from the vacuum and worshipped angels in the corner of reality." **Felix the Helix** in "The Quoted Mollusc"

But along the way our love became my love.
half dead but refusing to become extinct,
like the giant panda, probably
more trouble than it's worth,
some would say.
Another victim
of a beautiful malfunction
of the human attachment mechanism.

Since then,
nocturnal playing of Scott Walker albums,
haiku madness in the village hall and
a sense of dust at the edge of the carpet.

Now, I need a shot of what Asterix has,
a chirpy optimism and a useful potion,
or to be like Duckula and his chums,
impervious to love and with memories
that cut off every 30 minute episode.

So, good genie, give me a magic spell and
a cloak of invincibility with a logo to die for,
rid me forever of her feel, her taste,
a fugitive, enchanted masquerade,
and her jumble-sale Aztec-pattern dress.

Prose Poetry and a romance in the past tense

You know, people still ask me "What is a prose poem?"

Well, the rules are... only have rules if you need rules,
as in quantum chromodynamics and crossing the road.

The prose poem dispenses with
the illusion
that line-breaks
impart meaning.

Approaching Warsaw in '76
Listening to Santana
Her arm around me

The convergent history of
the poem and the sandwich
show that both remained essentially
unchanged until the 1960s, when
the prose sandwich and
the triple-decker poem
conquered post-war Britain.

The divergent history of
the poet and Ms Novak
has been responsible for
increased sales of Special Brew,
many excruciating poems, and
strange old times.

P.S. Instructions on composing a haiku
- write your best haiku
- lose seventeen syllables
- do something useful

Talking to my Plastic Buddha Blues

Tell me Buddha, how can I learn to be wise?
Not by listening to me, Sunshine!

Tell me Buddha, will we be O.K. after Brexit?
Would you be after being cuckolded by the village idiot?

Tell me Buddha, will I live happy ever after?
Snap out of it you prick, you're a big boy now.

Tell me Buddha, what sort of plastic are you made of?
Why phenol-formaldehyde resin.

Tell me Buddha, does phenol-formaldehyde resin hold the secret of the ages?
No, but if you shelled out on a modern polycarbonate or PTFE job you might be in luck.

Tell me Buddha, how about mahogany or.....*Shut up!*....Sorry

Tell me Buddha, if all life is suffering how can this be alleviated without the use of mind-altering chemicals?
I can recommend meditations on the Diamond Sutra or Felix's 'Ten Years a Mollusc'.

Tell me Buddha, who put the bop in the bop-shoowap-bebop?
Why Errol J Slocum, a little-known songwriter from Tallahassee.

Tell me Buddha, which star am I made of?
                    The third from the right Dave, now Good Night!

dave cook's walking sewer embankment blues

i walk the northern outfall stretching away to the south east
towards urban infinity above the unseen and ignored river
below above the waste of years to retrace history from bow
to beckton and from this wild elevation I look down at marble
memorials set in ranks among fern and london pride like an
armada in a green sea my only certain future which i survey
from this unintended serenity the heights of bazalgette where
ghandi once walked before me i see myself in the banality of
the chemical factory and you in the mystery of the wilderness
beyond the mud grey canal where we once found each other
children in the flow of time cyclists near and pass by as
if we inhabit different dimensions for they belong outside
of this silent parallel world where once i had dreams now
I have only dreams flow flow of people flow of history but
mostly of human waste both natural and artificial plastic
bottles diapers contraceptives shit and creative writings on
scrunched up pieces of paper once replete with meaning
now indifferent to their surroundings as they are to them the
metaphysical nature of the currents also carry wasted lives
and wasted words wasted hopes and wasted love hate is rarely
wasted it usually does its stuff where there was once the
fragrance of nitrogen oxides rancid offal and rarefied smog
the air is now bland the refreshing smell of strangeness
replaced by that of laundered expectations on occasions
I consider the option of escape the district line passes below
the A13 passes above but for now i will stick to anaerobic
solitude walking this earth and brick and concrete oasis of
possibilities

Divergent Evolution in Haikus

in brushstrokes my pen not showing, simply suggests gentle Hokai bird	
caged Hokai bird weeps restricted by convention she needs to break free	as brush must move on so the untamed bird follows the haiku responds
no sign of metre nor rhyme or cheeky humour sod this boring stuff	much like the sandwich the haiku never sits still it constantly evolves
what's wrong with a rhyme it's hardly organised crime and just about time	there's no business like show business, there's no business I know, 2, 3, 4
There once was a monk called Matsuo Who wrote far too many haikuo One day he said stuff! Enough is enough I'll drop this and start off anew-o	3.1415 9265358 97932....

Design Fault

What possible evolutionary advantage
is acquired by an organism whose members,
after a period of moist and sloppy exchanges
with another enters an absurdly protracted
and painful period of grief?

What is the nature of collective intelligence
that it can understand relativity and at least
calculate the workings of the quantum world
while spending this melancholic period
listening to Irish love songs and
old Paul McCartney records?

How come the wonderful creatures
that produce art, science, and music
of such beauty as 'Ellis Island' and 'Silly Love Songs'
live with the choice of emotionally dysfunctional
and greedy posh boys to rule them and screw up
the lives of their loved ones?

Perhaps by accepting the gifts supplied
by nature's adventures with DNA, like
the aardvark, MRI scans, ball bearings,
swanky loft conversions in Dollis Hill,
Bob Dylan's 'Like a Rolling Stone',
Wassily Kandinsky and the ukulele?
Oh, and the occasional moist and sloppy
exchange with another such organism.

Dream Soup

The silent scream that never comes
We search for something out of view
The serpent's poisoned bite that numbs

Arms flail but fail to beat the drum
But fall upon such sharp bamboo
The silent scream that never comes

In darkened streets I try to run
In alien skies where space craft grew
The serpent's poisoned bite that numbs

Pale underwater smiling sun
My skin is burst as wood grows through
The silent scream that never comes

The bolt is back – wait for the stun
To feel a love that I once knew
The serpent's poisoned bite that numbs

What was that game we had begun
The saddest dream, the search for you
The silent scream that never comes
The serpent's poisoned bite that numbs

Paradise Parasites

Long ago, when
Buffalo roamed the ancient malls of Stratford
Children, emerging fresh from war
Dared to dream and breathe others' air
Studying in upstart classrooms they
Read Sartre, Tolkien and quantum mechanics
Painted brightly with pigments and words
And, looking for freedom
Got lost in the rich flora of possibilities

Sensing an opportunity
Slowly, vote by vote
Bastard by bastard
The others began
To return
Replacing
Beauty with greed
Knowledge with vanity
And hope with dead leaves

Now, we have palaces
Overrun with new creatures
Magnificent Cows of Paradise
Bejewelled Masters of the Mint
Who spend humanity's sorrows
Wear other people's skin and
Carry empty hearts

Fire risk associated with the written word

My poems are soft green, my poems are also flaming crimson
after **José Martí**

Poetry can be inflammable and can inflame
Words can distinguish or extinguish

Items that burn include books of poems.
Just as forest fires free the land for new growth,
whole shelves of poetry in worthy bookshops,
in both up-and-coming and beyond-my-wallet areas,
in municipal libraries and homogeneous chain stores,
might best be incinerated to encourage new thinking.

Books on local history and "How the Tudors Lived"
are lifeless and dust-dry, paradoxically extinguishing
flame or passion and so may be utilised as
an inert stuffing for celebrity chefs or philosophy lecturers.

For fire to occur we require three things:

One – a fuel, for example, petroleum spirit,
certain paper products, such as
the tedious poetry of Waplia Dinsdale-Baguette
or that bloke Tracey Smith fancies.

Two – a source of ignition, which could be
hurriedly consummated sexual passion,
the intense hatred of human cruelty
or the delight of a well-chosen metaphor.

Three – a supply of an oxidant, usually air;
in the 1960s this was supplied by poets like
Ginsberg, Mitchell, McGough, Ferlinghetti
and by a new-found freedom.
At the time of writing however, air is in short supply all round.

Road-kill on love's superhighway

They say animals can smell fear, well I for one, can't.
Sadists home in on masochists, ants on thick sugary blobs.
The attraction of the folk dance club is to counter isolation,
provide meaning through art and possibly, find a mate.

Predators and crazies gravitate towards insecure people,
especially those who know that it's really always their fault.
Bastards are torn between suckers and other bastards,
in an oscillatory dance of parasitism and mutual grooming.
There are many forms of movements known as dancing;
some are trivial, some are unforgettable.

A certain type of female knows, yes just knows,
that this certain other type will be easy pickings.
Thus from the first courtship dance of hesitation,
to the last spasm of heartbreak,
he's as good as dead.

Urban Myths

So goes a legend in these parts
that spirits of the woods and hills
have fled the backwoods for new starts
among our dark Britannic mills.
Now urban ghouls spread fear around
the Cockney end of London Town.

Come two o'clock this night in Bow
twelve fairies led by knavish Puck
will turn black taxis into crows
and cabbies into bleating ducks.
Such tableaux have become routine
as jellied eels and pearly queens.

Nine Northern Outfall Sewer sprites
will journey on their tiny bikes
from Temple Mills to Beckton Heights
to scare nocturnal drunken tykes;
who, hearing squeaks or distant bells,
should ditch their cans and run like hell!

Will o' the Wisps now permeate
old Thames-side warehouses and slums
and lure lost souls to chilling fates
beside the O2 Stadium.
One apparition you may spot
- the ghostly Lady of Shalott.

In Wanstead Park once lovers strayed
to frolic in the ferns and fronds.
Now werewolves ply their fleshy trade

beside the ornamental ponds.
On sighting monsters, so I hear,
romantic notions disappear.

Lost in the misty Cornish Sea
enchanted sailors reappear
down moonlight-lit canals of Lea.
These spectres spooking Hackney Pier
can sail and fish and frolic free
at night with goblins or banshee.

This poet, witness to such scenes
of wild dark thoughts from wild dark dreams
remains an old-time rhyming mess,
though charged with images galore
of ancient wraiths and fear's caress
- he's lost his cred, no metaphor.

Somewhere 6am

Felix silenced the alarm clock with a lazy antenna. Slow to waken properly, he had been up most of the night sliming his heroic poetry on granite headstones, encouraging revolution and self-fulfilment in his fellow snails.	Polyphemus rubbed his one eye awake. Disturbed after watching 'Oh Brother' last night, he tried to cheer up with the thought of today's visitors. Odysseus and his crew are always lively company.
As the laboratory blinds were opened to the sunrise, shafts of misty light fell on the lifeless figure on the slab labelled experiment VF 213. "At last! Man has created life! Ha! The first artificial library assistant." Victor threw the high voltage switch.	Seeing Angela in soft-focus dawn, Danny smiled at the beautiful intensity and physicality now in his life, hardly believing his luck, until also recalling her children, his pregnant wife, oh, and 'Knuckles' Norman, soon to be released.
Milos Novak's first thoughts were memories of the Moon-cats and of Ilona and her android lovers, of the gaucho and the banker, of tearful lovemaking in mediaeval Birmingham and of the panda. So many years, so many creative-writing classes.	Cold, grey light, Raul clambers off the shattered raft and kisses the old jetty. The journey had seemed interminable, lost at sea, storms, hunger, so many dead. "Miami! My dream, a new life." Unaware of the sign 'Jaywick Sands 1mile'.

Having left to cool overnight in her workshop. Marta opened the oven to proudly reveal her crispbread Turner Prize entry representing urban innocence and lost faith. She felt exhilarated that that this year she really could be the winner! But, hmm, so good with cheese.

Dear Dave, I have devoted thirty-six years of my life to you faithfully and forgivingly; I have given you sons and my love. And who is it you obsess about in your poems? A sodding snail! This, you slime-loving creep is finally it! Your breakfast's in the cat.

Excerpt from "The Pasticheur"

based on "The Passenger" by **Iggy Pop**

I am the pasticheur and I rhyme as I write
I write like T S Eliot might
I write of men with nothing inside
Yeah, and snails with nothing inside
Nobody dead or alive I won't cite

I am the pasticheur, I live under stones
I write and ride on the Northern Line
I write a line like a Shakespeare might
Can I compare thee to a summer's night
Yeah, a dark and a slimy night
Justifiably compared to lignite
Singing la la la la lala la la   etc

We'll wear another's shell, we'll be the pasticheurs
On a branch of the Northern Line
We'll write a line like A M Klein
Avoiding any snails on the rails
Writing sonnets in slimy trails
The world of words is ours tonight

Oh, the pasticheur, he rides and he writes
Oh, the pasticheur, he writes on an August night
What does he write?
He writes of molluscs with an attitude
He writes of gastropods and thinks of seafood
He plays a Chopin ukulele etude
Let's take a listen to the air tonight
Singing la la la la lala la la   etc

Oh the pasticheur
He writes of astrochemistry
From a book he bought in Helsinki
He sees through his window tonight
He sees the stars that shine in the sky
Recycling recycled nuclei
Like carbon, nitrogen and oxygen
He sees the elements are ours tonight
He sees the elements are us tonight
So let's ride and write and rhyme and ride
Singing la la la la lalalala, la la la la lalalala,
la la la la lalalala, lalala!

Zarnesti Bran

Bran   Soil   Gravel   Rubble   Detritus
Dirt   Dust   Compost   Pile   Mass   Ground
Spectrophotometer   Waste   Hardcore   Infill   er?

Spectrophotometer   Galvanic cell   Diffraction grating
Wide base Interferometer   Scanning electron microscope
Thin film evaporator   Electron emission tomography
Spiny ant eater   Thin section polarised light microscopy
Dark field interactor   spiny what?

Spiny ant eater   aardvark   humming bird   cassowary
meercat   peregrine falcon   small furry animals   big cats
reptilian monsters   starry, starry night   ichneuman flies
lactobacillus   wassat?

a magic journey deep inside your mind   a shaft of sunlight
illuminating a valley   music touching the heart and the spirit
a tear of joy   the story of a world that you recognise
somehow   then the caress of a lover's hand that says
I adore you   Britart's expensive crap   the sight of
paradise in.........oh bollocks!

mission statements at dawn   imported plastic shit   Katie's
memoirs vol 87   timeshare in downtown Penissi   blokes
who've been everywhere apart from their hearts   greedy
bastards buying diamond-coated eggs to make them feel O.K.
corruption, avarice, mindlessness, misplaced pride, hate,
violence, couscous, ignorance and exploitation tempered
with......ambivalence

ambivalence?

male-female   right-wrong   love-hate   yin-yang
old-new   hard-soft   rich-poor   spiritual-earthed
timeless-timepiece   eternity-now   knife-kiss
breakfast-after   waking-again   with my
dream-partner

Compromisation

It might be wise to compromise
As new poetic fashion rules
That rhyme is only for old guys
And sorry clowns who play the fools

It's often wise to compromise
Encountering a maddened thug
Who strives to blacken both your eyes
After partaking of a drug

But compromise is rarely wise
While striving for dictatorship
As mighty empires fall, not rise
When tyrants lose their iron grip

Don't compromise on extra fries
When aiming to increase one's weight
Their calories are high as skies
Look down and see your waist inflate

When gazing in your lover's eyes
As pulses rise and wild hands play
It's not the time for compromise
Let urgent feelings have their say

Thermopylae's* wild battle cries
Gave heart to those outnumbered Greeks
Who's kings advise "No Compromise"
Pushed Persian armies up the creek

With socialists I socialise
But prize a little profit too
A small franchise in minced meat pies
I run outside of London Zoo

Don't compromise with Russian spies
With black bow ties in misty docks
And pray likewise, stay in disguise
Survey the scene from dark call box

There's Galileo Galilei's
Uncompromising repartee
A few white lies on Sun and skies
Might just have kept him safely free

Now compromise, no rhymes devise
At times the poet too must bend
Let me just talk of butterflies
And minimise, thighs, tries and eyes
So, eulogise the rhyme's demise
I think we've had enough of this!

(* One for the pedants)

In Praise of Philosophers

They think a bit and then they write
enormous quantities of words,
routinely clever and/or long,
some showing life to be absurd,
some claiming others to be wrong,
while always being in the right
and thinking new things all the time;
described in journals as sublime
no shades of grey, just black and white.

I love the wisdom of such men
with minds that never seem to fog.
No Neasden housewives in their ranks,
just existential pedagogues
from Oxford dons to learned Yanks
who's light flows free from fountain pens
to fill the shelves of academe
where learned scholars show esteem
and chuckle knowingly at Zen.

Since ancient times their wisdom taught
through ancient Greeks and Viennese,
ensures a quality of mind
to gather multiple degrees
and rise above the common kind;
the apogee of Western thought
(the Eastern kind is sort of crazy,
and best approached when drugged and hazy)
the envy of us simpler sorts.

Although their works seem so arcane
they come alive exemplified,
as boxes filled with undead cats
or brothers some of which had lied
and whether you are sane or bats.
These issue freely from their brains,
as do imaginary gods
with atheistic firing squads,
evoked to make their theory plain.

But what was that, you at the back?
Who say this is but futile crap!
A talking shop for spoilt brats!
My sly polemic bonehead trap
will put you down like puny rats!
Us clever bastards never crack;
our secret weapon is a stream
of opaque prose on mystic themes.
So stuff that up your anal tract!

Dinner for Two

May I suggest? To begin, dancing classes
On winter nights in a school gymnasium
Among wooden boards, trainers and worn leather
To burn calories and promote innocent intimacies
When the music plays and partners are chosen
Dinner is to be served

Somewhere in Stratford
Aperitifs of canned carbonated drink
Together with strange awakenings
On a bench seat smelling of oil and upholstery
Where savoury pledges may be shared
To excite but not satisfy the palate

First course here at Café Marinade
Among classic aromas of tea and bacon
The quality of which will not be noticed
As focus falls on brown eyes and fingertips
On little quirks and associated scents
This is the buffet car to who knows where

Main course in the Carpathian hills
Rich juices flavoured with Irish views
And danger, are to be relished alongside
Peppers to clean the palate in between
The discovery of unknown tastes
Among the perfume of wild ferns

Just desserts in the British Museum
Contrasting faint formaldehyde
With the organic chocolate gateau
Where guilt will be served over fruit salad
Seasoned with assorted pleas
Salt tears and kiwi fruit blend in the mouth

Many after-dinner coffees
fresh ground or instant
with or without little biscuits
in cups of different colours and sizes
in various locations
with or without feelings of regret
will be served separately
on different tables
with different people
in different worlds

Walt Disney Regrets

Bland America, wanting only a facade of
Apple-pie kids and pleasantness, hiding
Hand-guns and hatred
Such a pity, you craved only
Coloured shapes of just two dimensions
I could have given more

No pleasant rodent, Michael easily hid his
Darker therapy-resistant aspects
Vicious and bestial
Sordid attacks, moderated by
Minnie, love-blind polka-dotted lover
who, like you, looked away.

Behind an optimistic whistle, Jiminy concealed
Depression and drugs, and
Surprising strength for his size
Utilised in order to progress
Inappropriate obsessions with Bambi
Who at least had a loving Mom

More positively, Goofy
Ever the butt of tooth-related jibes
Worked tirelessly in solid state physics
While Dumbo studied the piccolo
And Dopey, mindfulness
this you too ignored

Begone forever, singing birds, saccharine young girls, heroes with smug chins, condescending pachyderms and royal assholes!

Come, oh come troubled ant-priest without faith, Hamlet – Danish bacon counsellor, Snow White's even filthier sister and any species, cute or otherwise, truly seeking existential meaning; I embrace you!

Don't I just hate Found Poetry!

Attempting to combine the Manx national anthem with a Waitrose voucher, Bertie Sprout produced a poem of quite breathtaking beauty.

> *My legs they are three,*
> *each one has a knee.*
> *There's 20p off all fish*
> *past its 'sell by' date.*

Mistaking his gas bill for a poem Dr Arnold Pi searched the document for tangential meaning and metaphor.

Period covered	*late Summer 1983*
What have I used?	*3.14159 kWh*
When did they get rid of	*Why the year that she gave you the*
British Thermal Units?	*elbow and went back to him.*
What should I do?	*You do not have to do anything as it*
	is covered by your present direct debit
What do I pay?	*Grief and a weird sense of isolation*
Emergency:	*Smell gas? Boiler Breakdown?*
Missing Her?	*Ring 131313 (not-answering service)*

Finally, the following lines were, astonishingly, found amongst the terms and conditions attached to an on-line bathroom fittings supplier; we think that it could be easily read in isolation as a poem.

> *Sophie believes in angels,*
> *she was told some years before*
> *by her Mum and Dad and crazy aunts*
> *that they guarded God's celestial shore*
> *(when not required to form a host*
> *or hover just above the floor)*

Amazing!

Six Degrees of Elmer Fudd

Elmer Fudd is looking straight at me and
is reimagining my very own woman
being caressed by a huge swan.

Elmer Fudd

I recall the story of Leda, I think of soft
toys.

1. Leda and the Swan

I think of myself stuffed, headpiece filled
with kapok.

2. Kapok

I am a character from Game of Thrones,
threatened by
steel-cold pressure on my guts, I am aware
of metallic bonding made possible by free
electrons.

3. Game of Thrones

With the unstoppable attraction of two
neodymium magnets,
I found myself walking towards her, even in
my sleep
I am drawn, obsessed, I am in the other
world

4. Metallic bond

Grass soft and damp underfoot, I am silent
hunting while being hunted

5. Desire

That pesky wabbit!

6. Bugs Bunny

How beautiful they are, the trains you miss

"How beautiful they are, the trains you miss" from
'The Magic Wasn't There' – lyrics **Clive James**

Rewound, replayed and lived again,
in small details, not broad-brush sweeps,
of passing joys and gathered pain.
Outside we smile, inside we weep.

These small details, not wide brush sweeps,
such memories don't fade with years.
Sometimes we smile, sometimes we weep.
Some feelings never disappear.

Our memories that dull with years
of trains we missed, of drinks undrunk.
Some feelings never disappear,
small snapshot scenes in heart-size chunks.

The trains we miss, the drinks undrunk,
re-screened by us on random play.
Small snapshot scenes in heart-size chunks
abandoned when you passed today.

Re-screened by us on random play,
the passing joys and treasured pain,
abandoned when you passed today.
Rewind, replay and live again.

A Geometric Construction of Perfection

Imagine a tetrahedron.
Imagine, an object at each vertex (or corner, if you like), four
in all.
Imagine now, for the sake of this poem, each object is a
person.

On the first corner we find Professor Kyoshi Matsuo, Japanese
engineer, famed in the design of an advanced bullet-train; a man
also of wide-ranging intellect and impeccable manners.

The second corner is occupied by Miss Constance Bumble, the
legendary "Railway Poet" of Little Wormley, who has brought to
trainspotting the beauty and inspiration of the spoken and written
word; her works having been translated widely in Micronesia.

Thirdly, we have Mr Hyram T Fudge Jnr who owns a fine "Casey
Jones" driver's hat, a considerable collection of Hornby Dublo
engines with rolling stock and other merchandise adorning miles
of imaginatively landscaped track and a large refrigerator stocked
generously with strong lager; Hyram resides somewhere in Iowa.

Envisage finally, Ms Wanda L Williams, a transient and slightly
fictitious former love experienced on a train journey from
Prague to Ostend; beautiful and not quite forgotten. Delicately
please, place her occupying our fourth, and final corner.

The visual and mathematical arts, science and technology,
beauty and humanity, appropriated expertly but just sufficiently
flawed for our needs are combined precisely at the centre of
our tetrahedron; behold the Perfect Railway Enthusiast.

The Unfashionable Animals of
Old London Zoo

When talking of creatures in Old London Zoo,
we speak of the tiger and penguin and gnu.
We scarcely consider the modest and lowly
and say they are ugly and think kinda slowly. But!
They quietly further themselves through their studies
in municipal centres at night with their buddies.
Some of the subjects they strive to advance?
Philosophy, poetry, science and dance.

The aquarium residents' "Poetry Please!" nights
convene in the dark, in the draught by the lid
The limpets and barnacles write like McGough might;
Appollinaire's style suits most fish but few squid.
Old winkles perform their work much like the Bard,
but ferrets and possums ape Monsieur Ronsard.

"Philosophy Forum" meets back of the pub,
where cavies and dingoes read René Descartes.
On Tuesdays the moles run the Wittgenstein Fan Club,
when termites and ants take old Ludwig apart.
The lugworms just love the works of Jacques Derrida
though scallops will place him among bottom feeders.

The spectrum of science these animals ponder
include the dynamics of gastropod mating.
The owls learn the workings inside a transponder,
fruit flies the genetics of multiple dating,
and bats astrophysics of stars that outlast yer.
While most know the universe now's getting faster.

On Fridays, dance classes are lavish and grand
where warthogs might rhumba and lampreys gavotte.
Imperceptibly strutting their stuff to the band
the barnacle formation troupe hits the spot.
Why then comes the spectacle last to arrive
ten starfish in sequins tap dancing Take Five.

So let it be known if you're warthog or flea,
you blossom by making the most of FE.

Instructions for the IKEA shrine 'Kamfors'

1. Your Shrine will need a good solid base, so find someone who is not there.

2. Assemble the Bric-a-Brac section, carefully arranging these small mementos of some significance. You pack should contain various rocks (5), brass bells (2), feathered paraphernalia (6), used railway tickets (3) and old receipt from the British Museum cafeteria (1).

3. Unpack the Hemling couch and drape it with the blanket labelled 'Warm Melancholy'; lay in it often and meditate on your higher power.

4. Using the Rimbo hooks hang a picture on the wall. This should be the only one you have as you wished you had taken more.

5. In one corner install Sadness; this is really the centre of it all.

6. Over the coming years assemble a mythology surrounding your chosen worship using places, people, times, stories in a believable history. Preferably real stories containing extraordinary and miraculous episodes.

7. Keep it a secret, holy place but every so often through the intermediacy of alcohol or poetry let someone have a glimpse inside.

Distance Learning

The underground, so I have found
is good for autodidacts who
can study subjects quite profound
with nothing that's distracting you.

At Chorleywood I understood
I'm just atomic Lego© bricks,
assembled before babyhood
with sly electrostatic tricks.

I studied Mill at Buckhurst Hill
and Descartes on the Northern Line
plus tons of tomes about free will
but just can't figure Wittgenstein.

While travelling to Becontree
I learned of quanta and the quark.
Equations used in chemistry,
I read just outside Belsize Park.

My guide to love in Leytonstone
turned out to be a heartless bitch.
So back to visit on my own
that little bookshop off Shoreditch.

For that Special Occasion

Dear Sharon, be my Valentine, today's a special day
Yes Archie take my cardboard token too
I thought our love was waning, past the point of no return
When February 14th hove into view
A Café Constance special-offer Valentino meal,
May stand in nicely for the love we knew

Between the flowers and the glitter ball
Between the industrial poetry and the orgasms
Reflections on love are desirable

With this nutritious pancake, I prepare myself for Lent
Through pulses and repentance for my soul
Each year I blend the eggs and flour with a pint of milk
And somehow throw the disc and catch it whole
Though I'm not sure what Shrove is and for forty days
and nights
I frankly tend to overfill my bowl

Between the making of the batter and tossing the pancake
Between the search for lemon juice and choice of topping
Reflections on Jesus can wait

Today let us remember those who died for us in vain
And those who killed and bled in useless test
We all look on as Eton's best (whose suffering is plain)
Parade with poppies proudly on their chest
We know we kill when asked to and weep our tears when told
But play the game believing for the best

Between the euphemism and the embarrassed cough in church
Between the prayers for our boys out there and the collecting box
There just may be a thought for the disenfranchised losers

Oh Dear, were can my colon be?
Blown away and stuck up an old dead tree
Now some MP will say something nice of me
without really giving a shit

P.S.

Oh, by the way! May I just remind you
that it was *you* who said "Forever"
when we loved on the bench seats
of my old Austin Cambridge
and we devoured 10p pieces
in telephonic marathons,
before you said "Forever…but"
in the British Museum café.

Since those days, so, so slowly,
our crazy, obsessive love
became.. only… my love.
I have however, no knowledge of
what your half is doing,
but, as for my half….
it's turned into something called 'Then'.

So thank you Then,
for coming to my rescue;
when a poem needs
a bit of poignancy

And today, conserved against
ravages of time and reality,
immune to the ageing process,
Then puts one finger up to change.

So fare thee well and good luck
from these other halves
to those other halves
wherever you are
whatever you are

YouTube Review of the week:
Lost on Translation (final 5 minutes)

"Shamelessly stealing the emotional power of Dave Cook's story, this clip renders the gut-wrenching beauty of unattainable love and turns it into sterile schmalz. The youthful scientist-poet of the novel has been substituted for, yes you guessed, an ageing Hollywood film star; the farcical illusion of acting being performed by Bill Murray and his only expression. You, meanwhile, are played by a nice enough young lady but really, not up to the job; she did, however, have me in tears."

Who Am I?

I am a husband, a father, a driver-about-town
I am a former drunk and a former embryo; I am also a former
passionate lover
I am a genetically programmed West Ham supporter
I am a collection of proteins, carbohydrates, lipids, nucleic
acids, minerals, hormones, ukuleles and sundry drugs; I am
potential compost
I am my dreams and my ideas, my hopes and my fears
I am composed of about the same proportion of metal parts
as a mandolin
I am a lover of quantum physics and women with a certain
look about them
I am the older man you see before you and surprisingly still alive
I am the creator of a gastropod with a mature appreciation of
philosophy
I am a pretty good chemist, an amateur geologist, a fair
physicist and a late-flowering ukulele-playing poet
I am a romantic crying out for beauty when I am not
concerned about the boiler
I am a chorus line of smiling dancers; I am grumpy as hell
I am marinated in cliches; I am other people
I am a subscriber to New Internationalist which I never read
I am the emotional-phenomenological me who cannot be
yet explained solely by physical measurements, by atoms or
molecules, by structures in DNA and proteins, by assemblages
of biological tissue, or by the firing of neurons
I am a wall-shadow, gone with the light
I am an organism that mostly doesn't know what it is going
to say until it opens its mouth or write until its fingers move –
Wonderful!

About 300 words on the word Love

I can mean so many things
I sneakily deactivate your peripheral vision and you don't even notice
I can make myself your number one priority and your emotions' sole focus
I am like a can of incense waved about automatically by priests. with little thought or scrutiny
I am one joyous and overwhelming insanity
I really am a knotted feeling in the gut
I am the secret need in dave cook that gives songs something to aim for
I hold out a hand and a heart without conditions
I am a tear on the face of a father
I magically appear, hover around a bit, then go like a wall shadow
I am able, like strong lager, to hold onto suckers long after the pleasure stops
I am not the same as half of 'our love' when your half is missing
I am a stolen April afternoon in Waltham Abbey
I am a word used to describe Jesus's feelings towards me before being threatened by Hell
I am, like the mathematical pi, not associated with any specific bodily location
I am also a sensation in my stomach, heart, head, mouth, genitals and fingertips
I sneak up on you when you don't expect it and sneak away while your back is turned
I have been a beautiful, tragic malfunction of the human attachment mechanism
I am like a play in which two clowns think they are heroes
I am a bunch of flowers on the 14th February
I am a sad teddybear metaphor for a lost childhood

I think I've been rather badly used by religious leaders and
abusive rotters
I have been known to surprisingly appear at parties, assisted
by alcoholic refreshments
I am a good night in, the complete home entertainment
package
I persist, even when lost, in the tedious poetry of aged
romantics

I wanted beauty: You gave me Nigel Farage

Dear Dad,

You asked me recently what gifts I would like for Christmas. I have been reflecting on the matter and decided to get something off my chest about what you and all your bulge generation mates have left for me and my chums. In the past....

- I wanted somewhere to live, you gave me an Xbox
- I wanted simply your education, you gave me a debt
- I wanted a job, you gave me zero hours
- I wanted a modern democracy, you gave me Corbyn and Rees-Mogg
- I wanted some 1960s optimism, you gave me a millennium bad dream
- I wanted brotherly love, you gave me fear of foreigners, and, like you before me
- I wanted a new world, you gave me a return to the Festival of Britain
- I wanted beauty and look what I've got!

So, Dad carry on enjoying your retirement, I will carry on working hard to fund you.

love Dave junior
P.S. I love you Dad but your mates are shit.

Poemisations #2

Science, Romance and Stuff

Science came into my life gradually. At 16 I got a job in a chemical factory where I was thrust into the world of wooden benches, night classes and mysterious bottles. After initial bewilderment I somehow became a half-decent working scientist. Now comfortable in that world I like to use science as naturally as others would use Greek myth or foreign holidays and intersperse it with the absurd and the very human.

The Importance of the Hydrogen Bond

Extract from "Cooke's Compleat Self-Educator"

Without hydrogen bonds we couldn't have
the tracks of the common (or uncommon) snail,
the snail itself nor its unfortunate cousin, the slug.
Neither will there be, luckily or inconveniently,
any other slimy secretion of your acquaintance.

We could have table salt but not tables,
let alone the parasitic but enigmatic lamprey
with its rudimentary nervous systems.

Without that special electromagnetic attraction
between protons and lone pairs of electrons
there would be no North Atlantic Drift nor
any ocean or body of water of any size at all.

This bond bears responsibility for the books of excruciating
poems of Veronica Grimsdale (amongst others),
for the anomalous behaviour of water
and for certain properties of romance.

The Hydrogen Bond brings intermolecular order,
stability to biochemical molecules and polymers,
and integrity to sundry biological tissues like
those of Tracey Smith, her skin, her taste of samphire,
and her faults which she has used efficiently in order to
provoke obsession, suffering and the tragic illusion of love.

Attractive or repulsive,
Electrostatics have much to answer for!

Angel Dust

The chemical symbol of Uranium is U

My love is mostly oxygen
as, in fact, am I.
But she is like a red, red rose
or scrummy, honey pie.

While I employ my carbon frame,
plus nitrogen and phosphorus;
all bonded with their tiny chums,
in merely building shelves for us.

My love is bright and pure as gold,
shining like the Sun.
A little proton-fusing star
creating helium.

But I, through chips of silicon,
indulge in heavy metal gloom,
partake of foreign molecules
and study physics in my room.

My love's atomic processes,
by rare uncertain chance,
emerge as someone wonderful,
about who planets dance.

She so excites my optic cones,
through iron, sulphur, iodine.
An angel made of earthly stuff
viewed through red and blue and green.

If by some transuranic luck
I found an atom no-one knew,
I'd call it Traceysmithium.
Then all the world will think of who
when seeing how some newish bomb
shines brighter than those made from U.

Atomic Number 20: Calcium

electronic configuration $1s^2.2s^2 2p^6.3s^2$

Calcium is a soft, brittle metal with a conventional view on the world. It dissolves in water releasing bubbles of a mysterious, colourless gas, said to be an antidote to trolls. The resulting solution, usually labelled slimey water, becomes more and more opaque as Timothy Eccles from Year 7 blows through it. This precipitate has been confused with both education and religion.

density $1.55g.cm^1$

Ores of calcium include attractive limestone hills, the Great Pyramid of Khufu and the bones of long-dead dictators. Calcium-containing minerals include Iceland Spar (Reykjavik – "Groceries R Us"), chalk and talk, Plastered in Paris and Mother of Earl. The most precious minerals of calcium are the kidney stones of virgins who have endured exquisite agony.

atomic radius 197pm

The metal is isolated by a derision-poemisation process and packed in airtight, humourless containers. It is not an attractive metal, less masculine than sodium with nothing like the brilliance of gold, but more honest than the *ignoble* metals. Nor has it the sexual allure of traceysmithium.

melting point $1117°K$, boiling point $1757°K$

Ions of Ca^{2+} mediate many cellular processes including slopping out and grass beating. Porridge is a good source of calcium for breakfast. Calcium is mostly created in supernovae and milk. One is a pleasant-tasting, readily available liquid, the other an unimaginably vast explosion millions of light years away.

thermal conductivity 200Wm⁻¹K⁻¹

Calcium is least abundant in the vacuum of deep space and most abundant on the planet Canine B, which is composed only of coral, teeth, bones, toothpaste and marble statues of the Venus de Milo. Charlie Cairolli, an Italian-English clown, born in 1910, was composed of 1.5% calcium. Louise Connolly (b.1950) contains more due to the possession of a hard, stony heart.

Pressure Difference

While showing little concern
about who Tiresias was, or is,
and some irritation as to
why he is, or was,
the white-coated figure
arranged his glassware in the lab
both artistically and functionally -
for where would we be if art
had no function?

If the Mona Lisa could not act as an effective draught-excluder?
If the twelve labours of Hercules did not include mucking out
the Stygian donkeys?
If the works of Anaïs Nin were non-absorbent?
If books of poetry did not darken with age in libraries demanding
gloomification?

One of the many arts in filtration is to assist it by a pressure
difference (ΔP) in order to reduce time (Δt) but also increase
mystery (Δ?).

Pressure differences can be seen to be at work
in the following artistic creations:

    (i)   Nena's 99 red balloons
    (ii)   Wallander's many cases involving strangulation
    (iii) Sinatra's Fly Me to the Moon
    (iv) Verne's 20,000 Leagues Under the Sea
    (v)   Marlon Brando hosed into the flames in The Fugitive Kind
    (vi) Tiresias J. Bloke's erotic adventure with a Buchner flask
          and a vacuum line as featured in the soon-to-be-released
          and much anticipated first poetry collection by Dr David
          C. Cook (Peewit Publications, 2018)

The Ballad of Erwin Schrödinger

I give you Erwin Schrödinger
Of wave mechanics fame
He followed life down many paths
Enlightened by his flame
For he found beauty in the world
That many folk don't see
In art, in life, in science too
A beacon burning free

In physics' gold uncertain age
He touched creation's heart
He saw in waves how atoms merge
How compounds fall apart
His instincts drew him to the pulse
Of logic's magic drum
And paved the way for DNA's
Discovery to come

Now women flocked like moths to light
To play and misbehave
As Erwin's path was strewn with love
Which Annemarie forgave
For he found beauty in the world
And love a sacred act
He somehow got away with that
Intelligence attracts

In physics and philosophy
In love, in life, in art
In Berlin, Oxford, Dublin Town
Remained a human heart

In fair pursuit of liberty
He found himself accused
In science he found mystery
In mystery his muse

So! Kongratz! Erwin Schrödinger
You seemed to have it all
In physics as a genius
In life you had a ball
You've left us much to think about
And physicists your tools
While you explore the afterlife
And gently test the rules

The Quantum-B-Biobox

The Quantum-B-Biobox measures your pleasures
To design an environment tailored for you
To fill with desirable personal treasures
Comes in purple and green or nice orange with blue

Probes, perfectly contoured, and delicate sensors
Connect straight to your psyche or soft fleshy parts
These wired or wireless info dispensers
Compute equations for your very own charts

The Blog-Me-2 function, through p-n-p junctions
Will find what you follow, be it Bieber or Fry
Reading tweet after tweet, no guilt or compunction
As you wallow in words which your heroes supply

Our Bunter-4 program, does chemorecepting
Just like those buds that inhabit your tongue
In busy cafés it's "Garçon!" intercepting
A waiter to order your favourite - fu yung!

The X-Fact-Adaptor, discovers your lover's
Erogenous zones and degrees of orgasm
Detecting crossed fingers made under the covers
Tells proper arousal from theatrical spasm

Protected by Firefox©, this brand new Biobox
Will work to enhance your life, mind and cuisine
So neat and supplied in a handy black bag that locks
It's never obtrusive and easy to clean

By the way......
A discreet on-off switch for the real connoisseur
Enables the user's life just to occur

Shaky Foundations

I

There is a perfect kilogram in Paris
made of platinum/iridium,
triple-layered and inertly sealed
protected from wear or accidental addition
in order never to change mass
but it did

There is a perfect woman
in a quiet street, east of London
crystallised in a memory as
an international standard ideal love
believed to be surely no fantasy
but she was

II

There is information on DNA sequences
in a world network of universities
where man can be mapped back
past apes and Jurassic mammals
to spooky Cambrian shrimps and
absurd blobs we call life, using
the faultless logic of base-pairing

Walter J Fergusson III wears a kilt and cries
whenever the band plays Flower of Scotland
stirring the two percent of his chromosomes
of Glaswegian origin and his romanticised heart
into a passion for someone else's country
Walter hates his dad but loves shrimps

III

Through a rigid three-dimensional lattice
of tetrahedrally-disposed carbon atoms
of high bond strength we have the diamond
Rare and expensive, it is the perfect gemstone,
the perfect abrasive, the perfect metaphor for
enduring love

Diamonds can be used to create wealth,
to subsidise murder and spoilt brats
and for sticking on stupid ornamental eggs.
They can show appreciation of special others,
but on the whole they are best burned

Three Poems about Iron

Part 1: Atomic Number 26

Iron has the most stable atomic nucleus, a melting point of 1538°C and a boiling point of 3134°C.

Iron is the main component of the Istanbul Express, the 2p coin and the rails used by the District Line. Sex was possible near the eastern terminus of the District Line, in off-peak times, until interconnecting carriages were introduced.

Timothy Eccles of Class 7B has covered magnetism this term.

Millions of tons of iron reside in the sulphide ores mined in Sulitjelma, Norway.

Part 2: In the Blood

Ferrous ions in haemoglobin drive our biochemical processes, including those within the brain, like those which thought up Minnie Mouse and the Corby Trouser Press.

Haemoglobin transferred sufficient energy to Louise Connolly's thought processes, some years ago, for her to steal my heart, trample it into the dust and stitch me up good and proper.

Although composed mostly of oxygen, the popular Tracey Smith contains 2.4g of iron.

Part 3: Iron Pyrites

on a hill above Sulitjelma
under fresh blossom,
your soft, pale skin astonishes me,
barely holding back the life within

schists, quartz veins and case-hardened steel drills
incongruous in the mine below

promises luxuriate above the rich soil
blossoms against blue and green,

love, as natural as the wilderness, as required by our DNA as,
bees' wings and motherhood

rooted in ancient rock, the grass has seen it before and laughs in
the breeze.....

Fool's gold below
Fool's gold above

Wonderful Tonight

As Shakespeare looked out towards Cassiopeia,
noticing the pale, misty halo around a new star
he imagined ghosts, dark grey stone castles,
troubled kings and murder in foreign lands;
he resolved to write yet more of kings and princes,
for our unelected rulers really do need
all the attention we can throw at them.

Tracey Smith, gazing up at the stars,
without considering chemicals or kings,
had thoughts of shoes and sang of twinkling bats.
Overhearing this, how Mr and Mrs Eliot laughed! "Oh!
her common vowels and excruciating diphthongs."
Seeing the possibilities in his latest work,
Tom inserted a suitably patronising passage.

From 54 light years distance, StarViewer 83M
looked past the nearby nebula towards a dim star.
He speculated about the existence of intelligent others,
but especially indulged in a recurring and fanciful dream
of an opposable thumb for holding a pen
with which to create fictional writing;
perhaps something comic or even tragic.

After a full day in the chemistry lab, Larry
observed the remains of a supernova
and thought of molecules and possibilities,
the evolution of planets and of emergence,
of hadrons, leptons, and the Velvet Underground
of obsessional human love and Penguin Poets
but, mostly, later that special night of
observing Tracey Smith on Facebook.

We are floating in space

About us
stars form and stars explode while
planets collide or planets grow
fed by dust and gravity
and mathematical precision

Since you, it has been
not a river, nor a flow of spacetime;
but it has been a circus parade
of multicoloured creatures
who, even now
sing songs
for us

They sing of what died in that long hot summer,
and laugh

The love I knew lives
side by side with
concerns for the Arts Council
and damp in the back-room while
seven billion others look up at the past
burning hydrogen in the sky,
dying, but hoping for infinity

La Chimie d'Amour

As I was contemplating the nature of my darling,
I listed all the elements that make her bright and charming.
Why, if I had to choose among the ones that give most
pleasure,
it's hydrogen and oxygen whose bonds I dearly treasure.

Her protein contains nitrogen and iron sits inside her haem,
while phosphorus in DNA helps to make her her it seems.
A-coursing through exquisite veins are peptide-bonded
alkyl chains,
and hydrophobic molecules partition to that perfect brain.

And when the moon's reflected light inspires romance in
the night,
I look upon those smiling teeth composed of fluoroapetite.
I also look upon awhile those wondrous parts which
me beguile,
composed of glycine, leucine, lysine, proline and a little bile.

Now my love, just cannot be, reduced to simple chemistry,
for she requires some physics too to drive her neat biology.
Those quanta with uncertainty I feel when she is near to me,
make me weaken at the knee through neurons' electricity.

But science surely can't explain my feelings when she went to Spain,
and came back with a distant look, which somehow caused
exquisite pain.
There's still uncharted mystery, of beauty that in her I see.
I've fallen for her carbon bonds and chemical geometry.

(Sing to tune of "Whiskey in the Jar" and make up your own chorus)

Shopping at Meyrin

Around Geneva

We have a shrine to the physics of creation in the hillside
Powered by electromagnets and liquid helium
Calculated almost as near to perfection
As Heisenberg allows

We have a palace to human peace and understanding
A cathedral for collective compassion
Populated by angels and devils
But mainly people

We have Europe's tallest mountains
Inspiration to poets and painters
Frozen and battered heroes
And triangular chocolate

But most of all
We have the neat convenience store
Where we bought some groceries
Coming back from CERN
Playing that CD

In Praise of Protective Clothing

The laboratory coat has protected me
from my cockney roots,
from car wax and football,
from Albert's new Austin and hernia news,
from the heat of impolite conversation,
from the grey of family advice.
We withstood them all, me and my lab coat.

The coat's white and sterile power
defended me from the sexual revolution.
With others suffering biological approaches
from newly emancipated young ladies,
I retained an uncomfortable virginity,
possibly unique in 1967.

Blokes in rock bands trumped
art school students who's
attraction to women topped car mechanics,
grave diggers and boys in the building trade
who all beat me, with my chemical factory,
and white coat.

Now, I am still protected from my enemies.
If reminded of their rules of grammar,
or the importance of one's schooling
or of a punctuation mark
or of Dante or Pitt the Younger or
other such blokes,
I put on my metaphorical lab coat,
reflect that quantum chemistry is important,
and love and snails are only emergent phenomena
among atoms,
and fly, me old son, fly.

Diamonds: Best when burned

Diamonds, tiny carbon tetrahedra, in perfect order
forged at immense pressure deep in the Earth,
transported volcanically to the rocks around us,
are now mined by lost souls for peanuts.
Diamonds are useful for providing
the vain and greedy with something
on which to waste their money.
Diamonds can burn in oxygen
to find humility in carbon dioxide.

Graphite, extensive sheets of triangles
made from buried dead plants, burns better,
after being dug up by singing Welshmen
and worthy people of other nations.
Graphite is also useful for writing
notes to loved ones in the margins
of sheet music and poetry or
better still, both.
Graphite also burns to give carbon dioxide
in satanic mills and cosy fireplaces.

Carbon dioxide, through photosynthesis
respiration and metabolic pathways deploys
carbon, in both tetrahedral and triangular forms
in the proteins, chromosomes, and hormones
of that familiar human shape from Surrey
in the small molecules which make her smell
of wood shavings and taste of samphire
and in the neurotransmissions of her smile.

In me, carbon enjoys its geometry in all sorts of biomolecules,
custodians of my foibles, ideas, regrets, and creations,
of feelings, emotions, pleasure, and pain, and
sundry other such gifts and fleeting enchantments.

Light-Emitting Diode

Thanks to Neils Bohr and the Carlsberg crowd,
we have reclaimed mystery
more beautiful than the offspring of ribs
more exciting than a clockwork universe.
We are all quantum uncertainty now.

But somehow, the cold LED light/
like soulless moonlight
telling me it is 2.45am,
a convergence of the semiconducting properties
of gallium arsenide and
electrons supplied to my home
through copper wires,
seems not of our world.

Nor can I believe my flesh, your flesh
is a product of Schrödingers waves
and Heisenberg's uncertain matrices
or my love and your love
emerges from atomic Lego pieces
covalent bonds and electrostatics.

Only too real though
is the time we missed.

Poemisation #3

The Life and Times of
Felix the Helix

Felix appeared sometime during therapy.

Felix the Helix Improves His Mind – 1.
The Gallery

This autodidact gastropod
will follow trails where critics trod
to view the masters' take on God,
or surrealistic dancing cod.

I favour Klee and Kandinsky
or Mondrian at sixty-three.
Geometry appeals to me,
especially spirality.

The pace involved in viewing art,
much slower than a shopping cart,
allows reflection for the smart;
who then ingest, digest, depart.

A snail can also get up close
to feel the pictures it likes most.
I've cohered to a Turner coast
and slimed a Hockney, I can boast.

My knowledge, now so multiplied,
a teacher I'll become, to guide
and educate snails far and wide
in beauty, art, and me, beside.

Felix the Helix Considers the Universe

What lies beyond the dustbin lid?
And can you touch the stars from there?
From winkles to the giant squid,
we all remain so unaware.

But I've thought long, and I've thought hard
on mysteries beyond my shell.
A snail among the avant-garde
my brain a small galvanic cell.

Now I have seen from inner space
and let my neurons wander free,
outside my calcite carapace,
beyond my common chemistry.

I've seen
Equations for the Sun's last day
All seven colours of a star
The code for love in DNA
Small silver tears on cinnabar

No better pastime for we snails
considering the Universe
than meeting in an upturned pail
to chew the fat and then converse.

And so to bed and so to dream
of molluscs famed in academe

The Unlikely Redemption of Felix the Helix

At Kindness Corner City Farm
the strangest animals reside;
five cobras who have lost their charm,
nine flatfish with a darker side,
French poodles that have bit gendarmes,
one mollusc with excessive pride.
Yes, Felix, master of the slime
adhering to the gift shop sign.
From there he runs clandestine trades
abetted by his closest aides.

His tentacles spread wide and far,
From cartels in the Middle East,
casinos in dark Kazak bars,
the services of Chang the Beast
and slime-jobs on World-leader's cars,
to lurid, multi-mollusc feasts.
All from a mostly unseen sign
with no-one to compete in crime;
except, of course, that slug called Sid
who lurks beneath the dustbin lid.

The battle of the gastropods
began when Sid slid through the door
to challenge Felix with sharp prods
and strutted 'round the gift-shop floor.
"Recall the twilight of the Gods.
Your days are up!" the slug did roar.
But Felix boldly took the stage;
he glared and shook his fists of rage.
At this display of metaphor
Sid slunk right out that silenced store.

This existential pantomime
made Felix reassess his ways,
for now he's changed, he's eschewed crime
he helps the farm to rescue strays.
And writes some rhymes in cursive slime
to cheer the kids on open days.
He even counsels irate slugs
and winkles who depend on drugs.
He meditates and works his quads
A modern, re-born gastropod.

Felix the Helix Addresses the United Nations

Felix ascends the podium, scans the audience, clears his throat

Fellow creatures,
I wish to speak on behalf of snails everywhere.
Today we face a rising tide of persecution
from some humans who have lost intelligence, and
without the neuronal efficiency we molluscs take for granted,
remain, like flightless birds, absurd.

But I ask those of you, who still are capable
of rational thought and empathy, Why?
Why cruelly crunch us underfoot?
Why give us painful deaths with
poison or sodium chloride?
Why remove us from salad plants?
Why shout "Get rid of that slimy creep!"?

We have become conduits for your existential fear,
victims of your immature revulsion and, yes,
euphemisms in your sexual shame.
Brothers, sisters face up to ephemerality
and your own slimy inner workings.

I implore you to evangelise on our behalf:

For molluscs feels much the way that you do.
They live and love and laugh and party too.
Although they rarely twitter, they enjoy a glass of bitter
and play the ukulele just like you.

A gastropod has rights like newt or peewit
with cultures as advanced as Greek or Brit.
They proudly swell their chest, emblazoned 'We're the Best'
on T-shirts that like yours so rarely fit.

So,
next time you're viewing patios at midnight,
look out for flowing script in shiny white.
Don't pass by with a shudder, you can treat him like a brother,
and a sister she's a real hermaphrodite.

Thank You

Felix the Helix, The Snail, The Myth

Too often mockingly likened to John Wayne, Felix decided he needed to acquire a greater range of facial expressions for his acting career.	Being no stranger to adventure but curiously traditional in outlook and habits, the life of the samurai warrior suited Felix well.
Looking incongruous even among Meccano models, Felix felt uncomfortable as a glamour model for the Large Hadron Collider.	After his first season with the Astana Ballet, the Kazakhs took Felix's untamed romanticism to their collective hearts.
Awaking from another of his "Mills and Boon" dreams, the melancholy of hermaphrodite love hit him hard that morning.	Described by many as a repulsive blob in a shell, only the wisest understood that they were dealing with none other than Felix the Helix.
As the sound of drums reached him, Felix found himself responding in an alarmingly erotic fashion; unfamiliar to a snail of such sensitivity and breeding.	"Volcanoes and snails just don't mix" Felix was heard to call as his good, but headstrong friends headed towards the smell of sulphur and French cooking.
Parking always having proved a tiresome irritation for him, Felix simply chose to ignore collateral damage when manoeuvring his strengthened 4x4 'Bigboy' TGX Snailcarrier.	"I may be but one small mollusc in an unknowable and meaningless Universe, but I have known love" Felix cried out to the vast emptiness of The Secret Slimestone Cavern.

A Tribute to Bob Dylan by Felix the Helix

Come gather 'round molluscs wherever you slide
On somebody's salad or washed up with the tide
The high place for humans is unoccupied
If the day for you is a'coming
Then you'd better start thinking or be battered and fried
For the rules, they are a'changing

This lowliest phylum derided and scorned
Will rise from its rock pools as poets are spawned
To praise octopus prophets whose thoughts have transformed
The lives of the squid and the bivalve
Our neurons are skimpy, but mankind be warned
That the game, it is a'changing

Come you clam, you mussel, you nautilus, you slug
Wipe the smiles off the mouths of those two-legged thugs
Who worship the heartless who take them for mugs
For their world is quickly eroding
There's room for a genus that never takes drugs
Yes the times, they are a'changing

The oyster so honest, the cockle sincere
Will rise to the thrones of those we once feared
No more to be covered with garlic and seared
At the barbecue's drunken excesses
We're slimy and shelly and blobby and weird
But the times, they are a'changing

Extracts from "The Quoted Mollusc"

Felix the Helix   2019-2020
English philosopher, revolutionary and lyricist

1   "Were I another species, or indeed phylum, I would eat pheasant, tripe, suckling pig or mussels with relish. As it is I graze on algae when fresh salad leaves are not available."

2   "For I will write an Iliad, an Odyssey, a Rubaiyat, in slime upon a thousand graves; for others to behold in awe."

3   "Slime, though your shell is aching, Slime, even though it's breaking." - *Song*

4   It can be a terrible thing, when a snail raises his voice.

On other creatures

5   Never underestimate a winkle.   *Mollusc World, Dec. 2017*

6   What an absurd creature – the slug – with only his spectacles to detract from his lowly and amorphous aspect.   *On Slugs*

7   The limitations of a slug are obvious and manifold.   *ibid*

On Existentialism

8   A snail condemned to freedom dares to dream of pavement cafes, absinth and a pipe.   *Nothing and Beingness*

9   I am nobody's son and daughter now, a shell alone in the universe.   *ibid*

10 I've slimed the highest walls and not found God; like Escher snails sliming to infinity. *Ibid*

11 As my mind watches itself, it manufactures beliefs more dangerous to truth than lies. *Tractatus Logico-Gastropodus*

12 Torn between two destinies, Felix lays his trail of slime in a melancholy fashion. *The Wall and Other Stories*

Tributes from others

13 "Felix the Helix is so much more than slime" *Boswell's Life of Felix*

14 The moment Felix decided to go to sea, he was destined to be but a broken shell washed up on the strand line; but with what a story to tell! *ibid*

15 Sliminess is a cloak you wear" was a song line Felix had used to devastating effect on the sexual desires of adolescent snails. *ibid*

A Snail defends his chosen Path

There lives a snail who daily rides, the Northern Outfall route
advancing snail philosophy, at stops on his commute.
His fame goes far beyond that path, and parts he cycles
through.
He's popular in Poplar *and!* well-known in Beckton too.

One fateful day, along the way, he met from academe,
a slug with views on things profound, of opposite extremes.
This slug was smart and wished to be the wisest in the land.
He saw that snail's wide-held esteem could thwart his future
plans.

Why then, of course, a fight broke out, their intellects engaged;
when snail dared criticise Descartes, the slug became enraged.
This heated mollusc likened slug to Heidegger's backside.
And so those thinkers battled on, but frankly they were tied.

First snail then slug, then slug then snail, appeared to come
out best
along that path from Woolwich East, to Stratford in the West.
It's tragic to see so much pride, ...spilt like blood in dust,
for snails and slugs are stubborn beasts, so strut and feud
they must.

Into their midst a small bird flew, suggesting change that day
"Why not smoke pot, expand the mind, and find a common
way?"
Begrudgingly the two inhaled, the joint that she passed round
and slowly those two mellowed, a friendship they had found.

But insights into deeper thoughts, can make deceitful dreams.
These wild and 'wise' perceptions may not be what they seem.
That wily bird incited both, to find the world they seek,
as snail and slug saw heaven's door, within an open beak.

Now let us not impugn the weed, that many folk hold dear;
Shall we just say our wily pair escaped that awful year.
The moral for philosophers and dodgy poets too?
Leave room for ambiguity, when you can't think it through.

Felix the Helix and the Recruiting Officer

I had a first cousin called Arthur the Slug.
He and I took a slide around a beer jug,
then weaved our way on to encounter some thugs
who worked for the Molluscan Army.
Two hulking great whelks came and stood in our way;
the ugliest smirked and smiling did say
"We're recruiting young gastropods like you today,
with our piper the winkle who'll charm thee."

"No thank you kind sir" we so calmly replied
"We've green leaves and carrots which need to be tried,
in the vegetable garden of Mr McBride,
to leave 'em all nibbled and slimy.
Beside if we were to enlist in your corps,
tomorrow we'd fertilise some foreign shore
while you are back here recruiting some more
who'll give up their lives 'cos they're barmy."

But those whelks showed their muscles to scare us a bit
"If you don't enlist we will beat you, you **its!
So sign on the line and pick up your kit,
while the winkle plays marches beside me."
But the snail and the slug are both clever and quick.
So modern, so subtle, we got out two sticks
and gave them some forschprung shillelagh technic.
Next time we will feather and tar thee!"

As for the young winkle we took up his pipes
and made a base drum of that helical tyke;
then dipped him in beer until he yelled "cripes!"
"Please don't tell my mother I'm craven."

So Arthur and I took a slow ramble back,
with beer and some lettuce upon which to snack,
as we toasted two whelks who enjoyed the crack
at the party two pacifists gave them.

(may be sung to the tune of "Arthur McBride")

So, Mr. Helix!

"So Mr., er sorry, Rev. Helix, welcome to NDA Laboratories. I see you are at present a common snail, *Cornu aspersum*, and you would like genetic enhancement?"

"Er, yes please my son. Can you explain to me the services you offer and what prices apply?"

"Well, Rev. Helix, may I call you sir or madam?"

"Yes certainly, but just plain Felix will do."

"Thank you sir or madam, our services range from minor cosmetic improvements up to the NDA Premier Executive Total Genetic Replacement Service".

"Could you do something about my smile perhaps?"

"Certainly sir, in fact our £24,000 basic gene edit would not only straighten your smile but correct the slight deviations in your eye stalks. As a bonus I think we can safely say that sir's little slime problem will be a thing of the past."

"If I were to push the boat out a little further could I become like one of those exotic Sumatran snails?"

"I can see that sir is a snail of good taste. Only a small edit would be necessary for such a closely related species. Take a look at our 'Exclusive Gastropod' range. You could not only look like this but be this for only £120,000, a small price to pay. Wouldn't you agree?"

"Er well, it would improve my chances with other molluscs but, may I be frank, I am not a poor snail by any means and was rather hoping for something more ..... dramatic!"

"Felix you are in the right place sir. Our executive range is extensive. How about a Bird of Paradise or a Snow Leopard? Or, if you could run to just a few more million, you could be George Clooney or Vladimir Putin. Both so noble, so macho, would you not agree?"

"Do you do Bart Simpson?"

"The cartoon character?"

"The very same."

"May I put it to sir that he is neither wealthy nor a reverend nor serious? Get out!!"

"It's a fair cop!"

Felix the Helix Cycles the Northern Outfall Sewer

"For this was the place where I dreamt without realising I was dreaming
where I found a sort of beauty without noticing there was beauty"
Felix the Helix

It's not often that a snail has time to reflect
on Victorian civil engineering in East London,
on the imaginary sexual encounters of chemist-poets
and on the rich romanticism to be found in sewage treatment.

I am cycling just feet above a superhighway of effluent.
This superiority protects me from contrived beauty -
above the crowds, above Faberge eggs and art auctions,
and above the rancid smell of Rolex watches.

Earth, brick, dust, dry grass and willow herb
history and industry along this artery of empire,
from Bow to Beckton, from Ghandi to Kubrick
"Oh Northern Outfall, how I love your detached majesty!"

Either side of my chosen path are the usual diversions;
mystical towpaths lined with mud-green flora,
the Prime Meridian celebrated with a municipal plaque,
and a timeless, anaerobic Palace of Joseph Bazalgette.

This urban corridor is decorated by graffiti artists,
and the residues of a boy's imaginations.
Recalling adventures among shrubbery slopes
and the dark-eyed girl from Railway Cottages.

Now you may be asking yourself-
"What is a snail to do when he runs out of sewer?"

Apocalyptica Helica

Apocalyptic days for snails
are those involving hobnail boots
or rains of concentrated salt
and tricky jars of damson jam

In times involving hobnail boots
and existential challenges
like tricky jars of damson jam
some may resort to therapy

Such existential challenges
can test a gastropod's resolve
while some resort to therapy
the bulk immerse themselves in prayer

To test a gastropod's resolve
the Gods have sent catastrophes
so we immerse ourselves in prayer
with closed eyestalks and shut-down minds

The Gods have sent catastrophes
like rains of concentrated salt
and closed eyestalks and shut-down minds.
Apocalyptic days for snails

Slime – A Poem in One Act

Cast

Narrator a bearded and quasi-theological figure

Felix an unusual and opinionated snail

Saint George upholder of modern tory values

Chorus an ill-disciplined octet of molluscs (Wallace Whelk, Sidney Slug, Suzanna von Squid, Otto Octopus, Clement Clam, Nellie Nautilus, Maurice Mussel and Winnie laWinkle)

Act One

Narrator is seated to one side on a blue plastic milk crate. Felix enters, sliming in a linear fashion.

Narrator.	Felix enters, sliming in a linear fashion.
Felix.	I, distant relative of the octopus, cousin of the clam, declare the truth of Eightfold symmetry, the undoubted benefit of silence, and the paradoxical but logically inevitable non-existence of a vacuum.
Chorus	Do we look like we care? Well do we?
Felix	For I have searched both time and space for mysteries beyond my shell.......
St George	In comes I, brave Saint George! To fight the frightful snail

Felix	I say! I say! Hold on my man. Can you not see that I am armed with only a blend of scientific truth, artistic creativity and love!
SG	And for that you must die!
C	"This is the ending of the Age of Aquarius..... the Age of AquariAAAAS!" (Members of the chorus drink from cans and start shouting) "Kill! Kill!
SG	Take that! Lefty bastard. (Hits Felix with a large cylindrical object)
F	Oh why did it have to be a slug pellet? (Felix falls to the ground; St George removes helmet revealing a Nigel Farage mask)
SG	My work is done! Over to you Boris.
	CURTAINS for all of us

Felix the Helix's Cowboy Song

In a honky-tonk palace, lived a snail of the west
with his sweetheart called Alice, in her fine, bustle dress
They say he has no my name but we know that's not true
He's a gastropod called Felix, who blew in from Waterloo
Blew in from Waterloo

One morning a stranger came, a'slidin' into town
A slug called Sid from Slugville and he wore dreadful frown
He cried out that he's looking for a woman dressed in lace
Under which you will find no calcite carapace
No calcite carapace

He says Alice is our kinfolk, and I'm taking her back
for slugs belong in Slugville, in our comfy cul-de-sac
but Felix now had stepped right up, says "Here's what she'll do!"
She's coming back to live with me in a park in Waterloo
A park in Waterloo

Now Sid was not a fighting man, in fact he was quite soft
He said goodbye to Alice, and returned to clean his loft,
while Felix stayed with Alice, and though she fancied Kew,
they settled down together in a park in Waterloo.
A park in Waterloo

So let this be a lesson, if you're just a lowly snail
You still appear above the worms, on a sliding scale
And when you're in a honky-tonk bar in the west,
stand tall and stand up for the slug you love best
You're a mollusc of the west.

(*Sung to the tune of "Big Iron" by* Marty Robbins)

The Augury of Felix the Helix

For there will be a great wind and mighty deluge
And after even forty days and forty nights
The Earth shall know light breeze with soft rain
Which shall bring forth new growth in lettuce

Then truly and slowly shall come a great King
Adorned in a helical carapace of calcite
To rule over all the creatures of the world
Who shall build for him a mystic Alcazar

And he shall gather sages and seers from afar
To charge them with just one transcendental task
"Fashion for me a magical but inexpensive instrument
which I can master without exertion or aptitude"

And on the fifth day Felix shall appear before us
With his enchanted but reasonably priced device
To deliver a simple folk song, singing of love
For all mankind but especially young ladies

And verily did Felix travel throughout Walthamstow
Seeking the sublime E17 Ukulele Congress
For they will take any old slimy strummer
Let alone a celestially gifted mollusc King

Felix's Unfinished Covid Chronicles

Day 1:

Today I have decided that not since the Byzantine Empire has it been such a good time to be a snail. Both life in quarantine and cycling the length of the sewer embankment provide an airy aspect away from the contagion of others. The sense of distance from the human race is helped by the fact that snails do not normally have concerns about respiratory difficulties.

Day 2:

The bicycle has opened my eyes to a world of possibilities hitherto before unavailable to myself and others like me. Exploration and travel has not been available logistically, limited crucially by the maximum velocity a snail can attain on an even, horizontal surface. Following the discovery of this magnificent machine my life has been transformed.

Day 3:

From the re-entrant tuning of the ukulele to the internal debates among statisticians, my knowledge grows daily. Perhaps I shall be like that bloke from Star Trek that increased his powers after encountering a magnetic space storm to become god-like. Or perhaps not.

Day 4:

Since Leviticus 11: 20-21 there has been some confusion about what insects one can and can't eat and, indeed what insects are. Reportedly, skewered locusts have been served for royal consumption.

Also reportedly, hermaphrodites gain little pleasure from sex. Don't believe a word!

Day 5:

Observing behaviours in the modern world, I have decided that people can be classified as either slug or snail. Slugs are, ugly, selfish, wilfully ignorant, destructive and know things to be true; whereas snails are beautiful, caring, respectful of learning, creative and open-minded. I stand before you a shining example of the latter, Lycra-clad and mud-splattered but constantly seeking cosmic truth and exciting new mucus-based beauty products.

A hiatus has descended on my international modelling career but, not to waste an opportunity, your favourite common but uncommon snail is working hard on looking even more fabulous.

Day 6:

Set in the pre-apocalyptic, dystopian present, the human race is awaiting judgement by unknowable gods. To ward off the massive meteorite of terrible consequences heading for the Earth, the Prime Minister is placed on a mountain top delivering an address which will surely save the planet – "We are all in it together. Excuse me the royal Martian rocket awaits."

Day 7:

Phew! Seem to have avoided said meteorite. It's such a nice day out there, perhaps I'll do a spot of gardening!

Epitaph

*"The World began in the Sea of Slime and will end in the Final Crunch;
but in between, some time to rhyme, have sex and a little lunch."*

Felix the Helix

www.ingramcontent.com/pod-product-compliance
Lightning Source LLC
Chambersburg PA
CBHW030501100426
42813CB00002B/302